# THE SCIENCE MUSEUM
# BOOK OF AMAZING FACTS

# DISCOVERIES

## BEVERLEY BIRCH

## ILLUSTRATED BY TIM ARCHBOLD

Hodder
Children's
Books

a division of Hodder Headline plc

# Contents

# Discovery

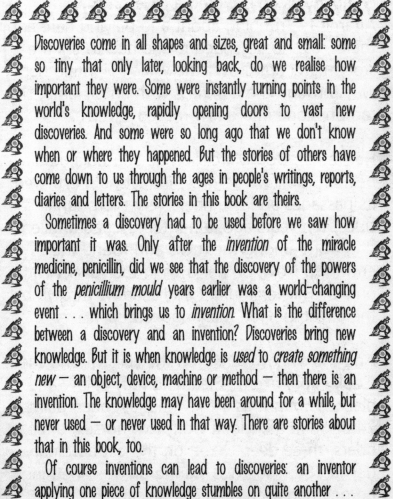

Discoveries come in all shapes and sizes, great and small: some so tiny that only later, looking back, do we realise how important they were. Some were instantly turning points in the world's knowledge, rapidly opening doors to vast new discoveries. And some were so long ago that we don't know when or where they happened. But the stories of others have come down to us through the ages in people's writings, reports, diaries and letters. The stories in this book are theirs.

Sometimes a discovery had to be used before we saw how important it was. Only after the *invention* of the miracle medicine, penicillin, did we see that the discovery of the powers of the *penicillium mould* years earlier was a world-changing event . . . which brings us to *invention*. What is the difference between a discovery and an invention? Discoveries bring new knowledge. But it is when knowledge is *used* to *create something new* — an object, device, machine or method — then there is an invention. The knowledge may have been around for a while, but never used — or never used in that way. There are stories about that in this book, too.

Of course inventions can lead to discoveries: an inventor applying one piece of knowledge stumbles on quite another . . .

# BISON ON THE CEILING

They might never have been found, except for small Maria. She was keeping her father company as he explored a cave on their farm at Altamira – 'running about and playing here and there', as she described it (she had to tell the story many times over the years). Lighting her way through the darkness with an oil lamp, she ran on alone into a low-roofed cavern ...

Her father, Don Marcellion de Sautuola, had been in the cave before – in fact he'd explored its passages and chambers very thoroughly since, ten years ago, a hunter rescued a fallen dog from among the rocks and found the entrance. Now, on her own in the cavern with only the flickering light and shadow thrown by the oil lamp, little Maria looked up.

And there they were – on the ceiling! She cried, 'Look Papa, oxen!' Gleaming red, yellow and black, as bright as if they had just been painted, 24 bison in a circle, a wolf, two horses, three boars, three deer ... Yet, on this extraordinary day in 1879, she was staring up at something no one had seen for 17,000 years.

Her father was delighted. Though he'd been in the chamber before, the roof was so low that he'd had to crawl. He'd never looked up! But now, because Maria was so small – so short ...!

All his knowledge and instincts told him that the paintings were very, very old. But he was in for a terrible disappointment. The paintings were too bright, too fresh-looking, the experts of the day announced. They must be fakes – an attempt at blatant fraud! No such paintings had been found elsewhere, so why should anyone believe they were by prehistoric artists?

De Sautuola died nine years later in 1888, his daughter Maria's discovery still dismissed as fraud.

But over the years similar paintings were found, mainly in France. And some of them could be precisely, definitely dated, because very old rock deposits formed *on top of them*. So the evidence mounted up, and one by one the experts changed their opinions.

In 1902 they finally accepted that those paintings Maria found in the cave on her father's farm at Altamira in Northern Spain were our first sight of Ice Age prehistoric art.

Sadly it was fourteen years too late for the disappointed Don Marcellion de Sautuola.

# CAVALCADES OF ANIMALS

Children also found important Ice Age cave paintings in France. About 60 years later, in 1940, four shepherd boys stumbled on the caverns and underground passages of Lascaux in the Dordogne region of France. There, in the echoing darkness that winds on and on through the limestone, magnificent, mysterious paintings and engravings cavort across the walls and roofs, vibrant in red, yellow and black. A stampede of beasts gallops towards the deep hollows of one chamber; four gigantic white bulls, outlined in black, loom up in another; smaller animals throng between their legs; horses trot along the walls, stags poise, tense. In the very deepest caves there are lions, and in one hole, a great bison rears to the attack, though wounded.

One of the boys who discovered them, Jacques Marsal, later became a guide there, and delighted in showing visitors these sights, just as he and his friends first saw them. People who have been there say that, standing in the ancient silence of the caves the images seem so alive that you hear the thunder of their hooves, even smell their hides ...

# WHAT - AND WHY?

But dad, we wanted Mickey Mouse

The Lascaux paintings also date from 17,000 years ago, in Ice Age Europe (the same as those at Altamira). More than 200 painted caves have been found in Europe, mostly in France and Spain. Among the pictures of animals are also other shapes – dots, grids, arrow-heads, zigzags, rectangles, series of curves nesting inside each other, like symbols and codes. And there are also some that are part-human, part-animal.

What do the paintings mean? Why were they done? What was happening while the artists worked? We still don't *know*, though experts have many ideas. Were they a kind of hunting magic? Experts think not, because we do know

(from animals' bones found broken up by tools) that in those days people weren't hunting and eating the kinds of animals shown in the paintings. Are they religious or ceremonial? Or decorations for a great, central meeting place? One expert reports that in some religious ceremonies today where people go into a trance, they first see symbol shapes like those found among the drawings of animals (zigzags, arrowheads, grids). Then the images become stronger and more powerful, taking other forms. So could it be that the prehistoric cave artists were in a trance while they painted?

Other scientists have investigated the cave echoes and shown that those places with the most powerful resonance – where the sound rebounds and swells from the walls and ceilings – have most paintings. So did people choose the caves for singing and chanting? Small heel prints have been found near statues in one cave; were children playing as artists worked? It's anybody's guess ... and perhaps we'll never work it out. Or perhaps some day, somewhere, someone will make a new discovery that will throw new light. This book is full of stories like that – one discovery building on an earlier one, to reveal something startlingly new ...

# INSPIRATION IN THE BATH

Soaking in a nice hot bath can be relaxing and calming and perfect for setting a person to cosy contemplation of life's mysteries. It can also provoke illuminating insights. There is a story that around 200 BC, the Greek Archimedes was idly watching how the water rose up the bath

when he settled down into it, and it struck him that a solid object (his body) *displaced* an amount of water when it was immersed in it. Or to put it another way: his body took up space in the water, pushing the water out of the way for it – and the amount of space it took up was shown by the height of the water in the bath rising. At the moment he realised the significance of this – the story goes – he shrieked, '*eureka*' ('I have found it'), leapt out of the bath and streaked down the street stark naked, pursued by a frantic servant. (The story doesn't say where he was going.)

So why was was he so excited? Well (the story goes on), the king, having ordered a new gold crown, was convinced his jeweller was cheating him, and asked Archimedes to prove it. Now, how do you find out what a crown is really made of, when the surface you see is shiny gold, and the crown feels good and heavy as a solid gold crown should? How can you tell whether or not it is really just lead inside, sneakily masked with gold?

Fortunately for the suspicious king, Archimedes' bathtime contemplations came to the rescue. It was easy enough to weigh a piece of metal,

and Archimedes already knew that a piece of lead of a particular weight, was *larger* than a piece of gold of the *same weight*. So, the clue was in finding out the size of the crown. Now, comparing the exact sizes of things is simple enough if your two objects are easily-measured shapes. But a crown, with fancy twiddly bits posed a rather different problem.

## EUREKA!

Which is where the bath comes in. Archimedes realised you can work out the exact size of an object simply by putting the whole thing in water – and *measuring the amount of water displaced by it*. So he could take a piece of pure gold that *weighed exactly the same as the crown*, and measure how much water it displaced. If the crown was also pure gold, it should displace *exactly the same amount of water* as that piece of gold. But, if the crown was partly lead (not so precious – and cheating the king who had paid for gold), then it would displace *more water* than the pure gold piece.

If it hadn't been for this brilliant insight, the king would either have had to put up with his nasty suspicions, or lose the crown by melting it

down or cutting it open to discover what it was made of. Archimedes had discovered a precise way of testing metals, and kings and merchants alike – not surprisingly – found his technique remarkably useful. Of course, it could be used on other objects too, and was – not least to test how big a load a ship could carry in the water.

## SLEEPLESS GOATS

His goats wouldn't sleep at night, so he was getting no rest. Frustrated, the young Ethiopian goat-herd named Kaldi watched the energetic animals closely and saw they were eating the fruits of an unknown tree. A small, red, cherry-like berry. Intrigued, he tasted some himself, and found they made him, too, feel peculiarly wakeful.

Or so the story goes ... This was supposed to
have happened in 850, and is how coffee was
discovered (it is brewed from the seeds found
inside the red fruit). But there is a question over
the legend: Kaldi probably wouldn't have coped
with eating enough of them to have an effect,
for coffee berries are horribly bitter. But it is true
that a drink called coffee *was* discovered around
the time mentioned in the legend, and the ever-
green coffee bush did develop originally in
Ethiopia. Plants were taken from there to other
countries, particularly Arabia, Egypt and Turkey,
where coffee houses became popular. So maybe
the legend has more than a grain of truth?

## SKY WATCHER

A delighted description of what the sky really
looked like through a telescope fell like a bomb-
shell on the world in 1610: it showed people
that the centuries-old beliefs about the universe
were all wrong. Galileo – a Professor of
Mathematics at Padua University in Italy – had
heard about telescopes being made in Holland.
You could use them to see distant things clearly
– and so, being a skilful instrument-maker, and
intrigued by the idea – he at once embarked on

building his own. Instead of looking through his telescope at land or sea, however, as others did, he decided to look at the sky.

## THE MOON AND ALL ABOUT IT

Nothing was quite as he – or anyone else – had imagined. For centuries people had argued about what caused the pale area of the heavens known as the Milky Way. Now Galileo saw that it was millions of stars. People thought the Moon was as smooth as a mirror. Galileo clearly saw its rough, rugged surface, 'full of hollows and protuberances', he wrote, 'just like the surface of the Earth itself, which is varied everywhere by lofty mountains and deep valleys,' and he made beautiful ink sketches to show this. He also discovered four moons orbiting the planet Jupiter.

Ah so, it's not true that the moon is made of cheese

Most exciting of all – he saw clearly that the Earth is moving round the Sun, *not*

*the other way around*. This was appalling: the Christian Church taught that the Earth was fixed – unmoving at the centre, the heart, of the universe (so, of course, it was the most important thing in it, at the heart of God's creation). The Sun and the planets merely revolved around the Earth.

Now here was Galileo, with delight and boldness, shattering the beliefs of centuries. The Professor of Philosophy at Padua was too afraid of what he might see through Galileo's telescope, and refused to look.

## STARRY MESSENGER

First, Galileo wrote a short account of the planets and the Moon, called *The Starry Messenger*. He didn't say much about the Sun and the Earth. But later he wrote a book about how the universe works, asserting that the Sun is the centre of the universe and does not move, and the Earth is not the centre of the universe, and does move. It was published in 1632, and it made the Church authorities furious. It was blatant, defiant heresy, flying directly in the face of their teachings! They put Galileo on trial before the Church court – the Inquisition. Under

threat of torture, Galileo said he didn't really believe what he'd written. His book was banned, and Galileo spent what remained of his life – eight years – imprisoned in a secluded house near Florence. Two hundred years passed before the Church lifted the ban on the book; a further 160 years before (in 1992) the Pope, the head of the Roman Catholic Church, finally pardoned Galileo, saying that the Church was wrong to punish him all those centuries ago.

# HEART AND BLOOD

The heart is the seat of a mysterious life-force – 'vital spirits' – allowing blood in merely to draw on the 'spirits'. This was how scientists at the beginning of the 1600s viewed the passage of blood through a body. It was an English doctor, William Harvey (later doctor to King James I and then Charles I), who turned all this on its head.

In 1628 Harvey caused a revolution in the study of the human body. Doctors were dissecting bodies and describing what they saw inside, but their investigations were horribly clouded by the ancient teachings. Bedevilled with ideas of 'vital spirits', no one, until Harvey, was really trying to

discover *how things worked*. Harvey was not content with just a description of what things looked like; he wanted to know how everything fitted together, what they were there for, what they actually *did*. So – very new and daring then – he did experiments. He investigated pulses in healthy and ill patients, watched the circulation of a live snake, observed what happened when he tied something tight round people's arms and legs. And he concluded that the heart is a wonderful, exquisitely efficient, *pump*. A muscle, he announced boldly (never mind those mysterious vital spirits): the muscle contracts and expands (alternately tenses and relaxes), in a regular action *in order to pump the blood around the body*.

From the heart it is pumped into the arteries that carry the blood out into the body and on into the veins, from there into the principal vein, and back to the heart.

He couldn't see how the blood got from arteries to veins. This would be understood later in the century with the magnifying power of the newly-invented microscope to help other scientists see the tiny blood vessels linking arteries to veins. With their microscopes, they were able to complete Harvey's discoveries. Yet extraordinarily few important corrections have been made to the pattern that Harvey discovered, without a microscope to help him, over 370 years ago.

He wrote his conclusions in a book that appeared in 1628, and a great many scientists didn't like it. The ancient ideas still sat firmly in too many minds. Just a muscular pump! No vital spirits! No more than a living machine! It created a sensation, and during the decades that followed, a flood of other writings proclaimed for and against. In the end, though, the overwhelming truth of it put paid to the opposers. Doctors and scientists didn't look back: Harvey's revolutionary approach pushed

them forward – study, analyse and experiment to reach your conclusions. Don't build elaborate ideas without foundation. Find evidence and proof ...

One immediate practical result was to prove right those doctors (such as field surgeons dealing with wounded soldiers) who were warning that people would die if left to bleed ...

# STRANGE ANIMALS

It was described as a kind of cat, very strange, about the size of a hare, the head like that of a civet cat; very short front paws – about the length of a finger, with five small nails or fingers, like a monkey's paw; two enormous hind-legs, which it walked on; a long tail, like that of a long-legged monkey. The creature sat on its hind-legs and clutched its food with its paws, like a squirrel. And strangest of all, the female had a pouch, big enough to take a man's hand. Inside were the young, sucking at the creature's nipples – tiny creatures about the size of a bean, though perfectly proportioned, so that it looked as though they were growing out of the nipples.

A weird fantasy animal? No – this is how Pelsaert, a Dutch explorer in 1629, recorded a European's first sight of an Australian kangaroo.

## AND FEARSOME BEASTS ...

Marco Polo returned to Venice just over 700 years ago after years of journeying in the East.

What tales he had to tell! Four-legged serpents, their mouths huge enough to swallow a man with a single gulp! And a unicorn, very large, not much smaller than an elephant, ugly, with a single black horn protruding from the middle of its forehead, and its huge, heavy head carried sloping to the ground. People in Europe pictured the most fearsome beasts and monsters. But Marco Polo was describing (can you guess?) ... a crocodile, and a rhinoceros.

# THE CART-HORSES AND THE SPHERES

Two bronze hemispheres clung together like a great metal globe, each hemisphere harnessed to two carthorses – each pair of horses straining, hooves slipping and sliding in an effort to pull one sphere away from the other. The Emperor and his court watched this tug of war, fascinated. The Mayor, Otto von Guericke, harnessed two more cart-horses to each side. Still the bronze hemispheres stuck together. He added to more horses, and then two more, then more and more. Suddenly, with sixteen horses hauling at each one, the hemispheres sprang apart.

Though Otto von Guericke always did things with pomp and ceremony and a grand sense of occasion, this wasn't just entertainment for the Emperor and his court. In the square at Magdeburg that day, an important scientific experiment was being performed, to find out about *vacuums*.

In the hollow space between the two hemispheres, Von Guericke had created a vacuum by pumping the air out. With his tug of war he had shown that with this vacuum between them, the pressure of the atmosphere, the air, on the outside of the hemispheres was enough to hold them together against the muscle and weight of 28 horses. Only 32 could finally separate them.

It showed that the pressure of air against a vacuum was a most powerful force. Though this event at Magdeburg in the 1670s was only the beginning of the discoveries, the work would, in time, lead to important developments. One – 30 years later – was the invention of the steam engine. That was born out of the knowledge that if you make a vacuum in a cylinder (remove all the air from it) the pressure of the atmosphere could push a piston down the cylinder with considerable force, a force that could be harnessed to move or lift a load, turn a wheel or pull a lever ...

# THE SPEED OF LIGHT

Looking for one thing sometimes leads to unexpected discoveries about quite another. So it was in 1676, with the speed of light ...

For several centuries great minds from many countries had been trying to find a way for people to make an accurate measurement, at sea, of how far they had travelled east or west round the world. We call it a measurement of *longitude*. One way was to try comparing your position with the orbits of planets and their moons, such as Jupiter, viewed from different parts of the world. For the purpose of recording and charting this, an astronomical observatory was built in Paris, filled with men of science from all over the world. There they trained their telescopes on Jupiter's moons, watching their paths, timing how long it took them to orbit and counting the number of times their small shapes vanished behind the shadow of giant Jupiter in their midst.

In 1610, Galileo, with his telescopes (see **Sky watcher** *page 18*) had shown that there were 1000 eclipses of Jupiter's moons each year, and that they happened so regularly you could set a watch by them. He drew up tables of each moon's expected disappearance and reappearance, a kind of astronomical timetable. As the years went by, all efforts were directed to making this knowledge more detailed, more precise, more useful as a guide to what you should see from anywhere in the world.

So it came about that in 1676 a visiting Danish astronomer, Ole Roemer, watching for the eclipses, found that all four of Jupiter's moons disappeared *ahead of schedule* when the Earth came *closest* to Jupiter in its orbit around the

Sun, and happened later than predicted when the Earth moved *farthest* from Jupiter. Were the predictions wrong? No, they weren't. Roemer found that the eclipses were taking place with absolute regularity, just as astronomers thought they should. What made the difference was the speed of light: the time when those eclipses could be seen from Earth depended on the *distance that the light from Jupiter's moons had to travel across space to reach Earth.*

At the time scientists believed that light travelled so fast it couldn't be measured. Roemer realised that efforts to measure had failed before because the distances tested were *too short*. Years before, Galileo had tried to time how long it took a lantern signal to travel from one hilltop

to another. But no matter how far apart the hills, he never found any difference in speed. Now, however, Roemer was watching across vast distances for the light of a moon to come out from behind the shadow of a planet. So enormous was the distance that differences in the arrival times of light when the Earth was nearer or further from Jupiter, were large enough to show. Roemer used the difference between the predicted eclipse time and the actual time he saw it to calculate the speed at which light was travelling. Amazingly, without all the equipment of modern science to help make the calculation accurate, he got it slightly under, but very close to, the 300,000 kilometres per second that is accepted now.

# ANIMALCULES!

There was once a linen-draper in Holland who used magnifying lenses to look at the cloth he sold. But he was a very curious man, so he made himself a magnifying glass to look at other things too, and peered into the puddles in his yard. He just wanted to find out what rain-water looked like, close up. Imagine the shock when he saw millions of creatures darting about in the water! He moved the lens away from his eye. Nothing but water. He put the lens back to his eye. There they were again: wriggle, squirm, slither, endlessly on the move, endlessly busy! A thousand times smaller – at least – than anything you could see with the naked eye.

Did they live anywhere else? He turned his lens on his skin, tree-bark, leaves, the holes in rotten teeth, his saliva, seeds, insects, even his own excrement. (He also nearly blinded himself watching exploding gunpowder.) Wherever he looked, there the miniature creatures were – and always invisible to his eye, revealed only when he looked through a lens. We know them as microbes, but then there weren't any books that explained what they were – for the simple

No! Leeuwenhoek you may not look at my socks with your microscope

reason that it was over 300 years ago (in the 1670s) and he was the first person ever to see them. His name was Anton van Leeuwenhoek, and he wrote excited letters to other scientists about his 'animalcules', so that they were swept up with his enthusiasms and started explorations with lenses themselves ...

But it never occurred to anyone then that these tiny creatures – found in and on everything – were actually *doing* anything ... other than just being there, being alive ...

# THE CASE OF THE EXPLODING BOTTLES

Popping corks in the cellars of the Abbey of Hautvillers in France troubled the cellar-keeper, a monk named Dom Pierre Pérignon. The corks kept flying right out of the wine bottles – pushed off by gas from the grape juice, still fermenting. It was towards the end of the seventeenth century, and there aren't records to tell us exactly what happened, except that Dom Pérignon tried to keep the corks in by twisting a twine cap round the neck of the bottles, covering this with wax. The wine went on

fermenting: Dom Pérignon was no longer faced merely with popping corks, but with exploding bottles.

But his wine delighted the taste buds of those who drank it – particularly at the court of the French king, Louis XV. By keeping the fermenting going inside the bottle, Dom Pérignon had, in about 1680, created a new type of light, fizzy wine that has become part of celebrations the world over – *champagne*. The problem of exploding bottles was solved some time later by using much thicker glass.

# THE AMBER FORCE

If you rub the natural substance, yellow amber, it will attract lightweight bodies to it. The Ancient Greeks noticed this, and believed it was because the amber took on an invisible fluid – a mysterious kind of life. Their name for amber was *elektron* – which is why our word for what they had discovered is 'electricity'.

Amber's ability to attract things to it was the sum total of the world's knowledge of electricity for more than 2000 years. Apart from treasuring amber (it is very beautiful), and using its special powers in ceremonies to foretell the future, nothing more really happened until Queen Elizabeth I's doctor, Dr Gilbert, began to study it in 1600. He revealed that all kinds of other materials – gemstones, fossils, stones, glasses and resins – when you rubbed them, also had the same strange power as amber.

# SPARK AND CRACKLE

By the 1700s, it was still just a peculiar, mysterious force, and fun to play with. People knew it sparked and made crackling noises when you rubbed certain materials with a piece of fur or cloth, and gave these materials the ability to attract lighter objects to them – or to push them away. They'd tried with feathers, paper, eggshells, soap bubbles, bits of bran ... They also knew the force gave off a prickling feeling, sometimes giving people a jolt enough to stun or make them feel weak for hours.

## PARTY GAMES

By the 1740s some travelling demonstrators hung people from the ceiling on silk threads and shot electric sparks through them. One rubbed a glass tube near a boy's feet, and made a spark fly to his feet, pass through his body so that his hair stood away from his head and a spark snapped from face and hands. Others played 'electric kiss' and 'electric handshake' with each other, making the electric sparks pass from one person to another. They shot the sparks like a flame round the gold frame of a mirror. For the amusement of the King of France, his whole brigade of guards stood in a line, and had an electric shock shot through them so they all jumped in the air. Another scientist made a line of monks three kilometres long leap about. Extraordinarily, no one seems to have been hurt. They didn't realise that electricity could kill.

# INTREPID EXPERIMENTS

Among all these intriguing experiments, some people were seriously trying to learn more about the spark. They started by just rubbing a glass rod to make the spark. But then they had glass globes made; you turned the globe with a handle against a pad set close enough to rub the surface of the globe as it spun. They tried passing the spark they made with the globes

through anything they could lay their hands on, just to see how it behaved: knitting needles, fire tongs, a poker, tea kettles (full of water and empty), gun barrels and cannon balls, a crowbar, salt, chalk, wood, bricks, water – even gold paint in the flowers of a china cup. They tried melting things with it – brass pins and needles. The found it could punch holes in thick board and set fire to dry gunpowder. They worked out how to make it travel along a wire into a glass bottle with metal inside it, collect it there and lead it out again when they wanted.

## THE BIG SPARK AND THE LITTLE SPARK

One of these energetic investigators was the American scientist, Benjamin Franklin, and he also wanted to know if lightning was the same as the crackling spark he made at home with his rubbed glass tubes and whirling globes. So out he went in a raging storm to draw the sparks down from the clouds with a kite and a wire, and lead the force into a glass bottle to take home and use in his experiments. He was lucky not to be killed. Someone else was, not long after, trying to test Franklin's ideas. But Franklin *did* learn that lightning was just a big version of the little spark from the globes.

# ALL AROUND THE GARDEN

Some things seemed to pass on the sparking force quickly. Others held it, and the force didn't pass on. Some years before Franklin's experiments, in 1729, an Englishman named Stephen Gray had started by just rubbing a glass tube, but noticed that the corks he happened to have in the end attracted small pieces of paper or metal. Next he put sticks at the end of the corks, then knobs at the end of the sticks, then balls tied to the end of strings. He hung a thread from the top window of his house, the lower end nearly touching the ground, and the upper end twisted round his glass tube. All of these attracted the paper just as well! So, he thought, electricity was something that could flow from one place to another without any matter that you could see actually moving. He imagined it as a weightless kind of fluid.

Finally he led the electricity on a kind of twine out of his room and right round the garden. That was when he made the next intriguing discovery. He suspended his thread first by twine loops, and found that the electricity *failed to flow* from one end to the other. Then he switched to silk loops. This time it worked. At

first he thought it worked with the silk because it was thin. But when he replaced a broken loop by a wire that was even thinner, the electricity didn't flow.

Did it work with silk loops because it was silk, not because it was thinner? He realised that electricity was leaking away through twine and wire loops, but not through the silk. Electricity, he concluded, flowed through some things and not through others. So in 1729 Stephen Gray, imaginatively trying this and that in his home and garden, started us off on our knowledge of what we call conductors (substances that electricity passes through easily) and insulators (substances that electricity doesn't pass through easily). Of course these names weren't used till much later.

But in spite of all that people were learning about the electric spark, they could not yet use it to light their homes, run machines, or send messages, as we do. The sparking force was conjured up, and gone again in a minute – fascinating, but it had no use.

# ANIMAL ELECTRICITY?

Twitching frogs legs led to the next discovery, in 1786. That was when Luigi Galvani, a scientist at the University of Bologna in Italy was experimenting with the sparking electric force. By chance he noticed that a dead frog's legs twitched if he touched them *at the same time* with two wires – one copper and one zinc. He thought there was a kind of special electrical fluid in the leg, and named it 'animal electricity'.

# THE FIRST BATTERY

The real meaning of what had happened was understood some years later in 1800, by another Italian, Alessandro Volta. He concluded that two *different* metals, separated by any moist substance, would produce a continuous flow of electricity – an *electric current*. He tried

wet paper stacked between metal plates. Then he made a collection of 'cells' (containers) filled with liquid chemicals and linked by different metals – usually copper and zinc plates in a dilute acid. The more cells he joined together, the more powerful the battery he made.

For the first time scientists could make more than short fierce sparks that flared and were gone. With a flow of electricity from a battery, they could begin the long series of experiments that led to the first important electrical inventions. But first of all, there was another part of the puzzle to be worked out, and it would be another twenty years before that happened... (*see* **Hidden connections** *page 51*)

# THOUGHTS ABOUT AN APPLE

A falling apple is said to have given Isaac Newton important thoughts about gravity – the force that pulls things to the ground when you drop them. It is one of the most famous stories about science, and is often dismissed as just a myth. But Dr William Stukeley knew Newton well – as an old man – and he recounted that

on a warm day in April 1726, the two drank tea together in the shade of some old apple trees. As they chatted, Newton told how, as a young man in the 1660s, he had sat like that and watched an apple fall to the ground.

Why? he had thought. Why should it always fall straight down? Why not sideways or upwards? Why always towards the Earth's centre? Perhaps, he thought there is some power that draws it.

Over the years he returned to this question again and again, and he came to the conclusion that, just as the Earth has a power that draws the apple, then it must be the other way round too – that the apple draws the Earth, there is a power in the apple too, and in everything in the universe ...

So began Newton's theories about the force we call gravity: the Earth's gravity stops us falling off the planet and the Moon from flying away into space. It also holds satellites or spacecraft in orbit round the Earth. The Sun's gravity, in turn, holds the Earth and other planets in their orbits. Everything – however small – exerts a pull of gravity on everything else. But this pull is usually too small to notice. Only when the pull of gravity is from something massive like the Earth, can it be detected.

This is what Newton began to think about when he saw the apple fall. And that all goes to show that you never know when important scientific ideas are going to pop into your head, if you are curious and interested enough and leave your mind open to them ...

# LIGHT IN ALL ITS COLOUR

As a young man Newton also wanted to know more about light. Scientists had known for a long time that light bends when it passes from one substance to another -- for example from air to water or water to air. You see this if you look at a stick in a glass of water: the part in the water seems to be a different size and at a different angle from the part in the air, because the light rays coming through the water bend as they re-enter the air.

Scientists knew you could bend light in interesting ways if you shone it through a glass prism – a chunk of glass with a number of flat surfaces at different angles to each other (like a jewel). So Newton began experiments with a prism ...

And he made a fascinating discovery. The prism seemed to bend light of different colours by *different amounts* (red differently from green light, for example). What would happen if he shone white light through the prism? In a dark room, in front of a round hole in the window

shutter (the hole about a centimetre across), Newton placed a prism, so that the sun's light shone through the hole, through the prism and on to the opposite wall of the room.

To his utter fascination, on the wall was not the white light, but an array of different colours! He had discovered that white light is made up of a mixture of colours: the prism had bent each colour by a different amount so that they spread out on the wall and he could see them. Rainbows are caused by this effect. Sunlight shines through water droplets that behave like Newton's prism: they bend the light rays, making the different colours spread into the glorious multi-coloured bow that we see.

# THOSE ANIMALCULES AGAIN!

Leeuwenhoek, discoverer of microbes, was long dead and the eighteenth century past the half-way mark when an Italian priest named Lazarro Spallanzani, a professor at the University of Reggio in Italy, became fascinated by the microscopic creatures that Leeuwenhoek had seen. There was a great debate going on at the time: does every living thing have to have parents, or can living things just spring into life spontaneously? The popular idea was that things *do* just spring into life. People thought that if you buried the carcass of a bullock, a swarm of bees would pop out; wasps and beetles would materialise from animal dung, mice and frogs slither from river mud and slime, maggots wriggle out of meat.

Spallanzani thought the whole idea of this 'spontaneous generation' of life was ridiculous. He had read the writings of a man named Redi who, a hundred years earlier (around the same time as Leeuwenhoek's adventures) had proved that flies had to reach meat for maggots to appear, had to lay their eggs in it. He put a dead snake, fish, eels, and a slice of veal into

open containers *and* into closed containers. In the closed containers, no maggots appeared. In the open ones, maggots wriggled away merrily.

Spallanzani was determined to test his own ideas out: he was convinced that animalcules (microbes) do not arise spontaneously either. When you find them on things, or in liquids, it is because they have reached there from somewhere else. He boiled up soups of seeds and beans to kill all microbes. He knew heat killed them because Leeuwenhoek had discovered it – drinking scalding coffee and finding the ones in his mouth were dead afterwards. Spallanzani sealed up the necks of his boiled flasks and showed that no new microbes ever appeared inside the flasks – unable to get in because of the seal.

He worked so hard to bury the idea of 'spontaneous generation' of living things. But in time it began to rear its obstinate head again, and it would take the discoveries of Louis Pasteur in the middle of the next century, to bury it for good and all ... (*see* **Spontaneous generation – again** *page 67*)

# Quiz

1 A small child discovered
   a) Champagne
   b) Animalcules in puddles
   c) Ice Age paintings

2 Galileo found out about
   a) The circulation of the blood
   b) The surface of the Moon
   c) Dinosaurs

3 Coffee was revealed by the antics of
   a) Sleepless goats
   b) Twitching frogs
   c) Sir Walter Raleigh

4 The speed of light was discovered when
   a) Ancient Greeks wore amber jewellery
   b) An astronomer looked at Jupiter's moons
   c) Franklin went to fly a kite

5 Leeuwenhoek was the discoverer of
   a) Telescopes
   b) Gravity
   c) Microbes

6　Who was imprisoned because of what he wrote?
　　a) Don Marcellion de Sautuola
　　b) Roald Dahl
　　c) Galileo

7　There was a famous tug of war at Magdeburg. It was between
　　a) A vacuum and some cart-horses
　　b) Archimedes and Spallanzani
　　c) A French king's guards

8　Demonstrators hung a boy on silk threads from the ceiling to show
　　a) That silk is very strong
　　b) That the boy was a circus acrobat
　　c) They could pass a spark through his body

9　Isaac Newton made his discoveries when
　　a) He was waiting for his goats to fall asleep
　　b) He shone light through a prism
　　c) He saw corks popping out of wine bottles

10　Champagne was discovered by
　　a) A French monk
　　b) An Ethiopian goat-herd
　　c) The Ancient Greeks

# THE LEADING STONES

Lumps of metallic ore could attract other metals to them. The Ancient Chinese noticed this, around 2600 BC. (It was like the discovery of the strange power in amber – its ability to attract light things to it – noticed by the Ancient Greeks.) What was more, if you let these lumps of natural ore move freely, they always swivelled round to point north–south, as if they had a mind and a life of their own. They were known as 'lodestones' – meaning leading stones – and the Chinese used their knowledge of them to invent the sailor's compass for finding their direction at sea.

# HIDDEN CONNECTIONS?

Amber, gems, glass: rubbing them gave them the power to spark and to attract things; lodestones – natural magnets – attracted things, and always pointed north–south. Was there a connection between these two – between electricity and *magnetism*?

By the 1800s some scientists were convinced there was, and were busy searching for a key to

the puzzle. The answer came, in the winter of 1820, in the hands of a Danish scientist, Hans Christian Oersted. He'd been looking for this connection for a long time, but the answer arrived quite unexpectedly one evening while he was giving a lecture on electricity and wasn't working on magnetism at all. He was giving a demonstration to his pupils: he passed an electric current (from a battery) through a wire held up on a wooden support.

Quite by chance, a magnetic compass lay on the table, pointing, as it always would, to north. When Oersted made the electric current flow through the wire, the *compass needle* swung round and pointed *away from north*.

There it was: that connection! A wire carrying an electric current, held close to a magnetic needle, but not touching it, made the magnetic needle move. When the wire was above, the needle moved in one direction; when the wire was below, the needle moved in the opposite direction! Inspired by Oersted's revelation, other scientists rushed to investigate further, and over the next decades the fact was firmly established: *electricity causes magnetism*.

# ALL KINDS OF USES

And scientists saw important possibilities: no longer just a tantalising subject for investigation, electricity could be *used*. Inventions followed: the electric needle-telegraph, used for passing messages: a flow of electricity caused magnetic needles to swing and point to letters of the alphabet.

They also discovered that if you coiled a wire in a certain way round a bar of non-magnetic iron and then passed electricity through the wire, you could turn the iron bar into a powerful magnet. Just as important, you could switch the magnetism off again, simply by stopping the flow of electricity. So you could bring a considerable power into existence, suddenly and at will, and just as suddenly destroy it.

This invention, the *electromagnet*, was at the heart of most of the earliest electrical inventions, such as the electric bell and the Morse code telegraph: in both of these, a flow of electricity caused electromagnets to operate – moving hammers and ringing the bell or shifting the levers that tapped out the message.

# DOES MAGNETISM CAUSE ELECTRICITY?

But the connection between electricity and magnetism was still mysterious, still not fully explored, and in 1831 the English scientist, Michael Faraday, began to wrestle with it. Ever since Oersted's discovery (*see* **Hidden connections** *page 51*), he had been fascinated by the link between the two extraordinary forces. He had done some explorations of his own, to learn more of how a magnetic needle could be moved by electricity flowing nearby. The French scientist, André-Marie Ampère had also discovered that *two wires* carrying electric currents could be made to attract or repel each other, just as if they were magnets!

Faraday's mind buzzed with possibilities. Could he do the opposite to what Oersted and Ampère had done: not use electricity to make a magnetic needle move or to make an electric wire behave like a magnet, but instead use a magnet or a flow of electricity to *create a new flow of electricity* in another wire, merely by bringing the magnet or electricity close to that wire, but not connected to it?

He took a ring of soft iron, about fifteen centimetres across, quite thick, and wound two separate lengths of copper wire (very good at conducting electricity) one on each half of the ring, leaving a gap between them. He connected the copper wire on one half to a wire he had arranged so that it passed over a compass. If an electric current passed through that wire, the compass needle would move – he knew that from Oersted's experiment. Then he took the two ends of the *second* wire, wound on the other half of the ring, and connected them to an electric battery, first one, then the other ...

Pleased to meet you, Mr Faraday YOOWWWWW!

The moment he touched the battery with the second end (thus completing the electrical circuit and creating the flow of electricity in this

second wire), the compass needle moved! Then it stopped. The current from the battery continued to flow steadily, but the compass needle didn't move again. But there *had* been a momentary flow of electricity in the first wire – passing over the compass – at exactly the moment Faraday sent the electricity flowing through the other, battery-connected, wire.

Faraday disconnected that wire from the battery, preparing to rearrange his equipment to try and get a better result. The moment he broke the connection from the battery (so that the current stopped flowing) the needle moved – briefly – again. There was no doubt: a current had definitely flowed again through the wire over the compass needle; and this wire had *no contact at all* with the battery wire where he had made and broken the electric current.

## ON AND OFF ...

He was on to something – though he was disappointed that the movement of the compass needle was so brief. Like any good scientist, however, he repeated the test again and again to be sure there was no mistake. Every time he switched the battery on, sending a current through the second wire, it induced a current – for a moment – in the first wire. Every time he switched it off, it flowed again – in the opposite direction. The electrical impulses only lasted a moment: if the battery current flowed continuously, the compass needle didn't move.

Now his disappointment changed to excitement. He grasped clearly what this meant. It was at the *make* and *break* of the electric current that it happened: something to do with the *changes* in the electricity created by switching electricity on and off in one wire induced an electric current in the other, strong enough to make the magnetic needle move.

Now he was on to the next stage: to find out if could he get the same kind of effect by using a magnet. He wrapped a coil of wire around a hollow cylinder of iron. This time he had no battery connected anywhere. Then he plunged a magnet into the centre of the cylinder wrapped with wire. Each time he did this, an electric current flowed through the wire!

New questions occurred to him: make a magnet move in and out – by attaching it to a crank fixed to a wheel which you turned, for example

– and perhaps you could turn the on–off electrical impulses into a continuous flow! The problem engrossed him for days ...

And one by one he solved the problems. It was a vital turning point. It meant that scientists now knew that, just as you could turn an iron bar into a magnet by passing electricity close to it (*see* **All kinds of uses** *page 53*), so you could make an electric current *that had not been there before* flow through a coil of wire merely by moving a magnet to and fro close to it. Or, what amounted to the same thing, by moving a coil near a magnet.

From Faraday's experiments came the understanding that allowed scientists to find more and more uses for electricity as the century progressed, harnessing the *combined forces of magnetism and electricity*, manipulating each to create and boost the other. Ways of using this knowledge often raced ahead of understanding what exactly was happening, and why. Even today, magnetism is not fully understood. But Faraday's discoveries in 1831 gave us the scientific principles behind all the machines we use to make electricity for lighting, heating and other purposes.

# ALL KINDS OF FORCES ...

Faraday drew his ideas together and concluded that electricity and magnetism are not just linked, they are different aspects of the same thing: indeed that many of the forces of the natural world – light and heat, for example – are different forms of this force: named *electromagnetism*. He began to see electricity and magnetism as 'lines of force' reaching out from magnets or electricity-carrying objects. For this all-embracing idea, Faraday is known as the father of electromagnetism.

# THE BEAGLE AND THE FINCHES

A certain Captain Fitzroy was embarking on a map-making voyage around the world in 1831, and wanted to take a scientist to record animals and plants they saw. A young student, Charles Darwin, got the job and turned out to be an excellent choice – energetic and hard-working (though he suffered horribly from sea-sickness), and a good companion. He made large collections of animals, plants, fossils and rocks, looked at everything very closely, and returned

from the five-year voyage with the seed of some world-changing ideas in his head.

Among many things, he had noted something particularly curious about birds – finches – on the Galapagos islands. Each island had its own particular kind of finch. Why? How did they arise? *Why* did they arise?

Having once entered his mind, the question gave him no rest. At home he began to write notebooks about all he had seen, found and thought. He searched long and hard in the work and writings of other scientists. He read everything he could lay his hands on – about plant and animal breeding and collections from all over the world, fossil hunters ... he even became a pigeon breeder himself, to learn more.

What were these ideas that so gripped him? He was reaching the conclusion that new kinds of animal *evolve* from earlier kinds. Small changes happen from one generation to the next, by chance. Some of these changes make an animal better suited – better *adapted* – to its environment: able to cope better with the climate, find food, ward off predators. Animals that have *not* been born with this change are

less likely to survive. So surviving members of the animal group carry the successful change forward, in their offspring, into new generations. Over millions of years the little changes have added up and new species of animals have evolved that are very different from their earlier ancestors.

There was a follow-on from this idea: humans and great apes shared a common ancestor a very, very long time ago – humans are just a very successful ape.

Is that great uncle Albert?

Over twenty years Darwin worked and worked at his ideas and collected evidence to support them. His book *Origin of Species* came out in 1859. In the meantime other scientists had moved towards similar ideas in their own work: they knew the Earth was very old, that there were lots of different species of animals in the world; fossils showed that animals and plants were once very different.

Nevertheless Darwin's theory had a stormy reception. In particular the Church didn't like it, because it challenged ideas about the creation of the world – in days – by God. But one scientist, persuaded by his mother to take Darwin's book on holiday with him, said, 'It sets the door of the universe ajar!' Though Darwin was not the only scientist to reach the conclusions he did, his book held such a wealth of examples, was so closely reasoned, so logical, it was an argument that persuaded most scientists. His *theory of evolution* made sense of the discoveries they were accumulating. Modern knowledge has changed and developed the details of what we know about the process of evolution, but that door opened by Darwin's great work was never closed again (*see also* **Tale of the garden peas** *page 69*).

# THE ARMY IN THE SUGARBEET

Rotting sugarbeet gave the first clues to what causes killer diseases. It all began in 1856, when a Monsieur Bigo asked the French scientist, Louis Pasteur, to help with a problem at his factory. Most of the time the process of changing beet sugar into alcohol was going fine, but, distressingly, some of the vats were turning sour. Louis Pasteur went along to have a look, though he didn't have any ideas, and he didn't know anything about alcohol manufacture and fermentation. But Bigo was the father of one of his pupils, so he wanted to help – if he could.

In Bigo's factory, Pasteur peered into the great vats of foaming sugar beet – the good ones with a vinegary, sweetish smell, and the sour ones with a disgusting stench and oozing grey slime. It left him none the wiser.

But he was inquisitive, and a careful scientist, so he took some liquid from a healthy vat and some from a sour vat, and because he was used to having a good long look at things through a microscope, he took the liquids back to his laboratory to do this. At once, with the power of the microscope, he saw the liquid from the healthy vat was swarming with tiny swimming globules, round and oval yellowish shapes with darker specks inside. From somewhere in the corners of his mind – something he'd read – he dragged a memory that there were yeast cells in

the mixture when sugar-beet juice or grapes were fermenting. These yellow globules must be yeast cells. But he also remembered that no one knew what they were doing there, though one scientist thought they were *alive*.

Fascinated, still watching them through the microscope, he saw one yeast grow strange little buds. Then the buds swelled and broke away – and became another yeast cell! He watched some more, and as he did so he became more and more convinced that the yeasts were alive, that they were doing something with their twirling and swimming and sailing along in bunches, chains, alone, together ... Were they at the heart of this fermentation process? Were they a miniature army ...?

## THE DANCING RODS

He had a look at the liquid from the sour vat. And what a shock he got! No nice yellow globules – just a vast shimmering world of black rods. Millions and millions of them – drifting and swirling in a weird vibrating dance that never seemed to stop. Much smaller than the yeasts!

He had a look at the healthy vats again. There was not a single black rod there. Caught by the challenge of the mystery, he wanted to study the dancing rods and couldn't see them properly all mixed up with the beet pulp. He needed something clear to put them in.

He tried sugar water, meat and vegetable soups, mixing and heating to kill other microbes, filtering his concoction clear, and then dropping in some of the black rods. But they never grew or multiplied. Nothing worked, until he made a sugar and yeast soup. He dropped a speck from the sour vat into a flask of this soup and kept it warm. Two days went by, and little bubbles of gas began to rise through the soup, and he saw specks in the liquid that weren't there before.

Under the microscope went a drop of the liquid. Yes! Millions of rods! From his single speck (his one colony of microbes), thousands of other colonies had grown.

And now a picture formed in his mind – of rods and yeast doing battle with each other. Yeasts in control meant good alcohol vats. But if the rods won the battle, a sour slimy mess ...

# SPONTANEOUS GENERATION – AGAIN

He thought: if microbes are causing alcohol fermentation, perhaps other tiny creatures in the world are busy making other things. Scientists at the time thought you found microbes on rotting things because rotting caused microbes to spring into life (that old idea of spontaneous generation again – the one that Spallanzani tried to bury eighty years before (*see page 47*)). Pasteur thought: maybe it's the other way around: perhaps rotting happens because microbes *make it happen*.

He did some experiments rather like ones that Spallanzani did before, and he proved without question that microbes do not spring to life spontaneously, but travel into things (matter and liquids) from outside – for example in dust in the air. He had the idea that there are different amounts of microbes in the dust in different places. To test this out, he took flasks of sealed, microbe-free soup to different types of place, opened them, sealed them again, carried them back to his laboratory, tested them for microbes. Out of *ten* flask opened in cellars in Paris, where

the air was still and Pasteur predicted there would be little dust, only one developed microbes. In a yard outside (dirty and dusty with traffic) *ten* out of *ten* grew microbes. On the hill near a small country town (cleaner air), only *eight* out of *twenty* grew microbes; on a higher hill, only five out of twenty. Finally he toiled up a mountain path to the sharp, fresh air on a glacier on Mont Blanc. Of the *twenty*

flasks opened there, only *one* went bad. He was only at the beginning of an idea that would in time transform medicine: that much disease in the world is caused by microbes invading human, animal or plant bodies, overwhelming and weakening them. Once doctors grasped this, they could track, catch, weaken and kill microbes (*see* **Those microbes again** *page 76*).

# TALE OF THE GARDEN PEAS

Pea plants in a monastery garden began to tell us the story of inheritance. A monk, Gregor Mendel, performed some breeding experiments in Austria over 130 years ago. He removed the flowers' stamens (which produce pollen) so they couldn't self-pollinate. Then he paired plants that had different characteristics – red or white flowers, smooth or wrinkled seeds, for example. Next he cross-pollinated each pair by brushing pollen from one on to the *stigma* of the other, planted the seeds that developed, and waited to see how they grew. At all stages he kept meticulous records of everything he did, and what happened.

It showed a pattern: somehow, parent plants passed characteristics to their offspring. He called this 'somehow' a 'hereditary factor', though he wasn't able to tell more about it. Today we call Mendel's 'hereditary factors' *genes*.

## CURIOUS COINCIDENCES

At the time, in 1865, Mendel didn't much talk about his work, fearful of how the Church would view it. Strangely, he was experimenting with peas at about the same time Charles Darwin was explaining evolution (*see* **The Beagle and the finches** *page 59*). Darwin's ideas rapidly became known all over the world; Mendel had trouble getting his published. He sent them to one scientist who didn't like maths and didn't want to look at the detailed figures showing numbers of offspring that inherited which characteristic! A local natural history society did publish it, but apart from this, other scientists knew nothing of his work. Darwin never had the chance to see it – a pity, because Mendel's discoveries filled in some important gaps.

Darwin knew something was being passed on from parent to offspring, but not how: Mendel's 'hereditary factor' explained this.

## REDISCOVERY

But in 1900 three different scientists, working in different countries, reached the same conclusions as Mendel. They searched the scientific reports for previous mentions, and each found Mendel's paper from over 30 years before. Unselfishly, they each promptly announced that Mendel was the first.

## THE JIGSAW PUZZLE COMES TOGETHER ...

The story of inheritance – of *genes* and *genetics* – had begun. But scientists knew only parts of it and still couldn't recognise the whole. One part came from microscope studies of the basic building blocks of living things called *cells* (such as skin cells and blood cells). Threadlike structures had been spotted inside the central core of cells, the *nucleus*. Another piece of knowledge came from investigations to find what substances are in the different parts of a cell. And then there was work on genetics ...

## THE CASE OF THE FRUIT FLY

One scientist was a bit doubtful about genetics, but in 1907 began to do breeding experiments with fruit flies. Their breeding cycle is two

weeks, so Thomas Hunt Morgan got quicker results than Mendel had from pea plants. He noticed that some characteristics tended to be inherited in groups (in the fruit fly, being male and having white eyes often happened together). He began sorting the genes for these characteristic into groups – putting into the same group ones that tended to occur together (the gene for male and the gene for white eyes), and ones that didn't occur together into separate groups ...

And he began to get the idea that *grouped genes* might actually be *physically linked* in some way – might be a piece of matter lined up in a row somewhere in the cell. Which is where those threadlike structures in the cell nucleus came in – we know them as *chromosomes*. Could this long thin thing be the site for rows

of genes? It was: By 1911 Morgan confirmed that genes are linked *because they are strung along the same chromosome.*

## BUT WHAT ARE THEY?

That still left the question of what a gene is actually made of. In the early 1940s scientists found that it is a chemical called DNA. They'd known about the chemical since 1869 – not long after Mendel's work – but had no idea before that it was connected to heredity or the chromosome. They now found that a gene is a tiny chunk of DNA, a kind of database, carrying messages in a chemical code to pass on to the next generation. Genes (a particular section of DNA) determine a baby's sex, a flower's perfume, the colour of an insect's wings.

## AND HOW DO THEY DO IT?

A little more than 50 years after Mendel's work was rediscovered, other scientists put the final piece of the jigsaw puzzle into place: they worked out how the chemical ingredients of the parent's DNA link up, pair up and then split off, carrying the chemical codes into the newly-created cells that form the offspring.

Nowadays there are constant advances in the way scientists can use this genetic knowledge – not least to understand hereditary diseases, and to breed strong healthy crops, suitable for different climates, able to resist disease.

# THE PETRIFIED MAN

The fossilised remains of a giant man were discovered by a farmer digging a well behind his barn. It was a relic of a huge species of extinct man that once inhabited New York State in America. Or so the newspapers trumpeted excitedly in 1868, and crowds of people rushed to look, paying a nickel for the privilege. Showmen and circus owners offered vast sums of money to be allowed to show the giant themselves.

OUCH! that hurt

And experts had a fine old time arguing about it. The Director of the New York State Museum thought it was just a stone statue, but still remarkable for being very old. Some, however, pronounced it a forgery and a fake.

It was – one of the boldest, most shameless scientific hoaxes in history, the brain-child of George Hull, of Binghamton, New York. He paid a Chicago stonecutter to shape the giant out of a five-tonne block of gypsum, sent the statue to his cousin, William Newell in Cardiff (near New York), who then 'found' it a year later, digging his well. The story hit the newspaper headlines. George and William put the giant in a ditch and pitched a tent nearby, and began selling a peep to the clamorous public.

Unfortunately for the pair, newshounds uncovered the fact that Hull had bought the gypsum, and then located the stonecutter. He described carving the giant, aging it with sand, ink and sulphuric acid, and punching 'pores' in it with darning needles. George Hull confessed, but claimed that he only wanted to make fun of churchmen who insisted that every word in the Bible was absolutely, literally true, including 'there were giants in the earth in those days'.

Nowadays you can see the fake displayed in a museum in Cooperstown, New York.

All this was possible because there was so little real evidence at the time about the path by which humans had developed from apes. So – for a time – the public was prepared to swallow it. *(See also* **The Beagle and the finches** *and* **Lucy** *pages 59 and 110.)*

# THOSE MICROBES AGAIN

Epidemic diseases due to microbes! (Pasteur was saying it *(see page 68)*.) How could something so enormous be caused by something so tiny, exclaimed the doctors. People were daily at the mercy of common deadly diseases. Six thousand people might die week after week, killed by the plague, cholera, typhoid, pneumonia and diphtheria. No one understood these diseases, and no one could stop them.

It was a country doctor in Germany who stopped those doubts for all time. In East Prussia, in the heart of farm country, a man named Robert Koch wanted to be an explorer but became a doctor, and was frustrated because he couldn't really do anything to cure disease. But his wife gave him a microscope for his birthday, and hoped it would help quieten his restlessness.

One day Koch turned his microscope on the dark, gluey blood from animals that had died from anthrax, a disease wiping out whole herds of sheep and cattle. At once the microscope revealed the swarms of microbes – like little rods – swimming in the sick blood. Following his explorer's instinct, Koch did a hundred tests and experiments and then a hundred more: he proved that the rod-like things were alive, that they multiplied, and were *never found in healthy animals*. They could survive in a shrivelled form until they burst into activity again. He injected them into animals and showed that the animals always then became sick – that the anthrax microbe, alone, caused anthrax.

## ONE MICROBE – ONE DISEASE

One microbe caused one disease. He had proved it. Now doctors and scientists began the hunt for microbes that had been slaughtering people year after year, determined to track them down, grow them, learn how they lived and died ...

# THE CASE OF THE OBSTINATE CHICKEN

A vicious poultry disease was killing one in every ten chickens in France. In 1878 Pasteur was studying the disease – chicken cholera – and was growing the microbes that caused the disease in a kind of soup. He injected this soup into chickens so that he could learn how the disease developed and, hopefully, how to cure it. Any chicken injected with the microbe-rich soup fell sick and died within days.

Now it was summer, and Pasteur went off on holiday, forgetting some chicken-cholera soup he'd prepared and left to one side. When he came back he was about to throw it away, for being old and stale. But for some reason he changed his mind, and decided to inject it into a hen anyway. In went a good dose. The hen became mildly sick, but recovered quickly – and then remained well. He injected more hens with the old 'soup'. They joined the first in strutting happily round the cages, smugly well. His brain aflame with what he dared hope was happening, he made a fresh brew of *live* strong chicken cholera microbes, strong enough to kill.

Every hen that had already had a dose of stale soup now got a killer dose of the new soup. None even became ill, let alone died. Now he dared the final test: he injected the fresh brew into another batch of hens that had *not* had a dose of the old soup. They all died. Pasteur understood immediately what this meant. He had discovered the method we use now to protect ourselves against many diseases. Microbes that cause a disease are weakened, then put into the body. This forces the body to develop weapons against them, so that it learns *in advance* to defend itself against live, strong microbes of the same kind, should they ever arrive. These preparations of weakened microbes are what we know as vaccines, and today we have vaccines against all the diseases that used to kill people in Pasteur's time.

Congratulations on your eggstraordinary discovery Mr Pasteur

# Chance

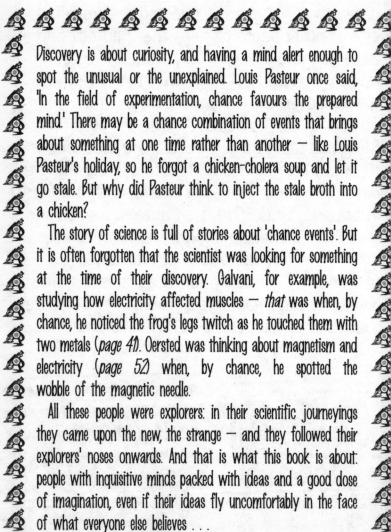

Discovery is about curiosity, and having a mind alert enough to spot the unusual or the unexplained. Louis Pasteur once said, 'In the field of experimentation, chance favours the prepared mind.' There may be a chance combination of events that brings about something at one time rather than another — like Louis Pasteur's holiday, so he forgot a chicken-cholera soup and let it go stale. But why did Pasteur think to inject the stale broth into a chicken?

The story of science is full of stories about 'chance events'. But it is often forgotten that the scientist was looking for something at the time of their discovery. Galvani, for example, was studying how electricity affected muscles — *that* was when, by chance, he noticed the frog's legs twitch as he touched them with two metals (*page 41*). Oersted was thinking about magnetism and electricity (*page 52*) when, by chance, he spotted the wobble of the magnetic needle.

All these people were explorers: in their scientific journeyings they came upon the new, the strange — and they followed their explorers' noses onwards. And that is what this book is about: people with inquisitive minds packed with ideas and a good dose of imagination, even if their ideas fly uncomfortably in the face of what everyone else believes . . .

# INVISIBLE WAVES

There are invisible electric waves that travel at
the speed of light. Mathematical calculations
led the Scottish scientist, James Clerk Maxwell,
to announce this in 1873, without any physical
proof at all, and without doing any experiments:
just maths – detailed, precise calculations – to
express Faraday's ideas about electricity and
magnetism being forms of the combined forces
of electricity and magnetism – *electromagnetism*
(*see* **Does magnetism cause electricity?**
*page 54*).

James Clerk Maxwell was an extraordinary
mathematician. He could use his skill not only to
express Faraday's idea, but also to predict that
the same *electromagnetism* exists as well in a
different form, as an invisible disturbance, a
kind of vibration, which moves – like visible light
– in waves. He calculated that it would travel at
the speed of light – 300,000 kilometres per
second – and pass through solid matter, gases
and liquids, and easily through a vacuum –
space from which all air has been removed (*see
also* **The carthorses and the spheres** *page
26*). This was an intriguing suggestion, thought-
provoking, believed by most scientists to be true

because of the brilliance of the maths, but nevertheless unproven.

But he was right – which just goes to show what you can do with maths! In 1887, eight years after Maxwell died, another scientist proved it. He

*I wonder what electromagnetism looks like*

thought, if there are electrical waves that *radiate through space* from one place to another, that vibrate through the air, then I must find a way to make electricity spark through the air and make these vibrations, and then try to detect them some distance away.

## FINDING THE INVISIBLE WAVES

His name was Heinrich Hertz, and his experiment was splendidly simple, brilliantly conceived. He knew, from others' work, that if you shot an electric spark across a gap between two pieces of metal in a certain way, the electricity surged to and fro across the gap. It happened very fast – about 500,000,000 times a second, and Hertz hoped that creating such a spark would cause strong vibrations in the air. So he made something to create the spark – a 'transmitter', a source of electricity connected to two large brass plates, with a gap between the plates. When he sent electricity across this gap, a spark jumped across.

To detect the disturbance in the air, he arranged his 'receiver' a few metres away – a circle of copper wire, also with a small gap in it.

And then he shot electricity through his transmitter, making the big spark jump the gap between its brass plates; at exactly the same time a tiny spark jumped the smaller gap in the receiver's copper wire circle. Yet he had seen nothing cross between transmitter and receiver. No doubt about it, electricity crossing the transmitter gap had been radiated as an invisible wave across several metres of the room, reached the copper-circle receiver, and sparked across its gap. Those invisible electromagnetic waves James Clerk Maxwell had predicted really did

exist. They became known as Hertzian waves, later wireless waves, because they needed no wires to travel along. We know them as radio waves.

# SIGNALS THAT FLEW ACROSS THE WORLD

A boy on holiday with his mother in the Italian mountains read about Hertz's work, and became obsessed with an idea: could Hertzian waves be made to *send messages through the air*, across countries, continents, oceans ...?

Scientists told him it was not possible to send the electrical waves more than a few kilometres – you just couldn't make them strong enough. It was just a young boy's dream! But in his home in Italy, the boy, Guglielmo Marconi, succeeded. He was just twenty when, in 1894, he began work in dusty attic rooms at the top of his house. First he sent the waves a few metres, as Hertz had done. Then from one end of the attic to the other, then to the floor below and the floor below that. Over the months he made them jump longer and longer distances between his transmitter and receiver, fiddling with batteries and bits of copper wire, sheets of metal from old water tanks, metal balls, tubes of metal filings, developing Hertz's original equipment, borrowing ideas from other scientists, changing them to suit his purpose.

Then he shot them from field to field, his brother Alfonso guarding the receiver, shouting out each time the surge of electricity sent by Marconi from the attic set the receiver's buzzer tingling. One day Marconi tried two metal plates wired to his transmitter. He arranged them this way and that, trying to make the signals jump further. One metal plate lay on the ground. By chance he held the other in the air. There was a sudden victorious shout and a frantic waving of Alfonso's flag. Way beyond the ridge, out of sight, the receiver's buzzer had buzzed. The invisible waves had flown across the hill!

# FURTHER AND FURTHER

And it was the metal plate held in the air that made the difference. Over the next six years Marconi worked and worked to get the arrangement right. He raised one plate higher and higher. He changed it for a copper wire, and called it an aerial (also an antenna). He buried the other plate in the ground. Week by week, month by month he sent the electrical vibrations across longer stretches of land and water. Finally he faced the challenge of 3200 kilometres of unbroken water – the Atlantic.

# BOUNCING BACK

Again scientists said he couldn't succeed because radio waves travel in straight lines. The Earth was curved, so radio waves passing any distance would shoot out into space. But Marconi did send them winging across the world in 1901, and at the time scientists could not explain how he succeeded. It was only twenty years later that they learned that although radio waves do shoot away from the Earth's surface, they are bounced back again by the *ionosphere* – layers of tiny electrical particles high up in the atmosphere, caused by the sun's radiation. Once they knew this, scientists could begin to use the ionosphere to manipulate wireless signals to travel as far and wherever they wanted.

# DUEL OF THE DINOSAUR DIGGERS

Just over 100 years ago some of the greatest collections of fossils were made by two men who were fierce rivals and loathed each other. They tried anything, however mean, to beat each other to a new find. Edward Drinker Cope and Othniel C. Marsh rushed to issue reports of their discoveries, never checking with each other. So, all too often, each named and wrote an account of the same dinosaur at about the same time as the other. The dinosaur thus got a Cope name and a Marsh name, and it took museums 30 years to sort out the confusion,

work out
which were
single species
with two
names and
which of the
quarrelsome
pair had
named it first.

Cope once
named a
fossil
*Anisconchus*
*cophater* (the jagged-toothed Cope-hater) and
the label still stands, a permanent joke about his
arch-rival, Marsh.

## THE BATTLE OF THE BONES

Cope dynamited his digging sites after he'd got
what he wanted – an outrageous thing for a
scientist to do. Anything to stop others (Marsh)
from finding scientific treasures that might be
buried there. Then he learned that Marsh didn't
do this, so he promptly moved in to search
Marsh's sites ... A fossil hunter offered to sell
important bones to Cope. Marsh sent the man a

fake message saying Cope didn't want them
any more, and bought the fossils himself.

He also humiliated Cope as he unveiled his
reconstructed *Elasmosaurus*. The creature had
an enormous neck as well as a long, tapering
tail. Two tails, Marsh gleefully pointed out: Cope
had mounted one tail at each end and didn't
know one end of a dinosaur from another!

Nevertheless, before they were finished, the
argumentative pair had between them
discovered and named 1718 new kinds of fossil
animals and packed several large museums with
dinosaur skeletons.

# THE CINEMA OF THE FANTASTIC

An accidental snarl-up in a film led to the first true cinema illusion – the original 'special effect' in fantasy films. The first director of these kinds of films was a Frenchman named Méliès, and in 1894 his equipment was playing up as he filmed in a square in Paris. The films kept catching, twisting and tearing. On one such occasion it took a minute or two to free the film and get everything rolling again. On the filming went.

Later, with the snapped pieces of film patched together, he settled down to project it. It showed a bus trundling along – suddenly no longer a bus, but a funeral hearse; women walked by; miraculously, they were transformed to men!

Of course what had actually happened was that while the film was mended, vehicles and people had moved on – pedestrians, buses and cars were no longer where they had been when the film broke; other things had moved into those positions. Joining the two bits of film together – one from before the break, and one from after – produced the *illusion* that things had simply switched from being one thing to being another!

Until then, Méliès had achieved spooky or strange effects by using theatre-stage tricks – smoke, trapdoors, lifts and swings. Now he had a vision of special *film* effects. First he did simple substitutions. Then he got better at it, and made things appear to be dissolving or appearing gradually or transforming slowly – first exposing the film with a white background, then exposing it again, this time filming an object or person. He had one actor play ten roles all at the same time by re-exposing the same film ten times.

And so, from this accidental beginning, imaginative techniques developed, like those used to create wonderful and scary illusions in films like *Star Wars* and *E.T.*

# UNKNOWN RAYS

A ray that passed through human flesh but not bones, and so could make a shadow-picture of the skeleton inside a living body – a shocking idea! Seeing inside people was a threat to privacy and one professor was so horrified at the sight of his own skull, a newspaper reported, that he had not slept a wink since. Others announced amazing uses: one man claimed to have taken 400 photos of the human soul.

This story began on a winter evening in November 1895, when a German professor, Wilhelm Konrad Röntgen, was – like many

others – busy trying to find out more about electricity and magnetism and the connection between them. He was investigating the fact that if you passed a current of electricity through a closed glass tube from which a lot of the air had been removed, part of the tube's glass began to glow; this glowing area could be moved by a magnet.

What caused the glowing? Here was a mystery that many scientists were trying to understand. One had found that if the tube had a metal-foil 'window' in it, the electrical rays could penetrate this and cause the glowing a few centimetres beyond the tube, outside it. Röntgen wondered if this might happen even when there was no metal-foil window. He covered his tube with black cardboard, closing the curtains to make the room dark. To test that his cardboard shield would not let ordinary light through, he turned on the electricity and passed a current through the tube ...

And he spotted that a piece of paper on his table was sparkling as if lit by a ray of sunshine. Caused by some kind of electric spark? Röntgen thought not – the reflection was too bright. And it couldn't be the rays he was already

investigating, because the sparkle was too far away. Some other ray – a kind of *invisible light* – must have passed through the cardboard shield round the tube and travelled invisibly through the air. He had no idea what the rays were, so he dubbed them X-rays, and the name has stuck ever since.

He found that these rays could pass through anything, though fewer pass through heavy materials like metals than through light ones like wood and paper. Very little got through lead, for example. And because X-rays can pass through anything, they can even reach a photographic film wrapped in black paper. Photographic film goes dark if exposed to any kind of light; the more light it receives, the darker it goes. If you put a photographic film on one side of a person's body and an X-ray machine on the other, the X-rays pass through the body and make an image of the body shape on the film (the flesh darker and the bones lighter, because more rays pass through flesh and fewer through bones). Within days of this discovery, doctors used X-rays to find a bullet in a person's leg. They took pictures of a human foetus inside its mother, a needle in a dancer's foot, and the skull of an Egyptian mummy,

without removing the bandages from the head.
One even watched pearl buttons pass down the
throat and round the digestive system of a dog!
They didn't yet know that too many X-rays is
very dangerous.

# MORE MYSTERY RAYS

Radioactivity first revealed itself on a cloudy day
in Paris – in a desk drawer. It was only a few
months after Röntgen had discovered X-rays,
and there was a ferment of activity to find out
about the mysterious rays and how they could
be used. Henri Becquerel was studying the fact
that some chemicals glow when X-rays shine on
them. He wondered if other chemicals might
*send out* X-rays if strong light, like sunlight,
reached them. So he tested this out.

He took a piece of photographic film and
wrapped it carefully in several layers of black
paper, to make sure that no ordinary, visible
light could get through and darken the film
(though X-rays would be able to get through).
Then he put a thin metal sheet on top of the
wrapped film, and sprinkled it with a crust of
chemicals, and put the film, metal sheet and

chemical out in the bright sunlight for several hours. Next he developed the film to see if the chemical had sent out any X-rays that had passed through the black paper and metal to darken the film. He tried with many chemicals, and found that only one made a shadow picture on the photographic plate – a chemical containing a white metal called uranium.

One day he prepared his experiment again. But it was a gloomy February day, the Sun wasn't shining, frustrating for Becquerel. His experiment would have to wait another day. He put his sandwich of black-wrapped film, metal sheet and uranium chemical carefully in a drawer, ready for the next burst of sunshine.

The Paris sky remained obstinately cloudy. By some strange stroke of fortune, a few days later he developed the film anyway, even though it had sat in the dark drawer for several days. The film showed the strong shadow-shape of the uranium chemical. The uranium must be sending out rays *all by itself*, without help from any X-ray machine or the Sun. Like X-rays, these rays had passed *through* the metal sheet and black paper and reached the film, but they were not the same thing at all.

Being a careful scientist, he did more tests. At the bottom of a cardboard box, he put a photographic plate, then some uranium, working all the time in a darkroom so nothing could be contaminated by ordinary light. He

It's either the uranium sandwich or an old cheese sandwich

closed the box, put it in another box, and into a drawer for two months, from March to May. The result was the same.

Becquerel had discovered radioactivity, though this name wasn't used yet. He announced the discovery of his unknown rays ...

# THE POWER OF RADIUM

A young Polish student named Marie Curie read about them and was at once aflame with questions. What were they? How strong? *Why*

did they happen? Did other substances, not just uranium, send them out? How to find out?

There was one way of knowing if the rays were present. Becquerel had shown that they made electricity pass through the air, and Marie could measure the amount of electricity easily with an electrometer, invented by her husband, Pierre. She collected samples of all the substances used in the school laboratories where she and Pierre worked, and tested them with the electrometer. Lumps, powders, mixed up, heated, cooled, wet and dry – she tried everything. She wrote down all the results, everything that happened.

A pattern began to show: whenever there was uranium in the sample, the electrometer showed strong electricity, which meant strong rays. Uranium is an *element*, one of the basic materials, such as gold, silver, carbon, iron, oxygen and hydrogen, which make up all substances in the world. Marie wondered: do other elements, not just uranium, also send out Becquerel's strange rays?

She tried them, one by one. And the answer was no – until she came to a grey metal called thorium. A new string of questions whirled in

her mind. Rocks, sand, soil? Off she set on a new search: if she was right about elements she should find that only rocks, soils or sand that contained *uranium* or *thorium* would send out the rays.

And she was right. She looked closer at the samples with the rays (by now she was using the word *radioactivity* – suggesting 'radiating rays'). She put a lump of black rock – pitchblende ore – on the electrometer. Enormous radioactivity! But it puzzled her, because she knew the rock didn't have much uranium or thorium. Then came another with vast radioactivity – much, much stronger than uranium or thorium.

Something else must be in the rock. An unknown substance, never before seen. A completely *new* element. It turned out to be not one but two new substances – the first she named polonium, after Poland, Marie's country of birth. The second was *radium*.

Where was it – and what did it look like? She and Pierre joined forces, and began the search. It was like looking for a single grain of sand in a whole bucketful, slowly breaking down the

pitchblende into
its different
chemicals,
testing each for
radioactivity
and throwing
away the parts
that were not
radioactive. They
got closer and
closer ... sackful
after sackful of pitchblende
was sifted, ground, mixed, heated, dissolved,
filtered ... The part left behind got smaller and
smaller until it was just a thimbleful. But it had
gigantic radioactivity – over a million times more
than uranium. It took Marie and Pierre four long
years to find radium, and separate it from the
pitchblende ore.

## A KEY TO NEW UNDERSTANDING

It wasn't long before it was discovered that
radium could be used to treat cancer: Marie's
discovery saved and lengthened millions of lives.
But it also gave scientists an immensely
powerful tool for *new* discoveries. They already
knew that elements are made up of building

blocks called *atoms*, but they thought atoms were the smallest possible pieces of matter and could not be broken down into anything smaller. Marie began to wonder if radioactivity was going on inside the *atom*. Perhaps there were even tinier pieces – particles – that moved around inside the atom? Other scientists later explored that idea, using the power of her radium – learning more about the atom and the enormous *nuclear energy* locked inside it. It was just the beginning of a vast new story of discovery with many chapters – one that is still being written today.

# EXTINCT – BUT ALIVE AND KICKING

It was a strange, blue–grey fish with strong fins on stalks, quite large – about two metres long – and not like anything the fishermen had ever seen in their nets before. It was 1938, near the mouth of the River Chalumna, in the Mozambique channel, and the peculiar fish wasn't just new to the fishermen. South African ichthyologist (fish expert) J.L.B. Smith realised it was a coelacanth. This was particularly odd, because coelacanths had been thought to have been extinct for 60–70 million years! Fossils had been found in ancient rocks, but no one had ever seen a living one. Smith named it *Latimeria chalumnae* after his fellow

ichthyologist, Courtenay-Latimer, and the river. One of the most extraordinary things was that the fish had not changed in all those millions of years. At first other scientists refused to believe Smith and Latimer's conclusions, because the fish was dead and rotting when it reached them, so it was difficult to see what it was really like. But eight more have since been found alive. Case proved!

Scientists have also discovered other 'living fossils': one is the tuatara of New Zealand, a lizard-like leftover from a great family of dinosaurs; the duckbilled platypus of Australia is another.

# Quiz

1  Lodestones are
   a) Early weighing machines
   b) Electromagnets
   c) Lumps of ore that attract metals to them

2  The theory of evolution was developed by
   a) Darwin after a round-the-world voyage
   b) Archimedes after his bath
   c) Pasteur in a sugar-beet factory

3  Which of the following are *not* connected?
   a) Pasteur and microbes
   b) Spallanzani and electricity
   c) Faraday and magnetism

4  The fossil of a giant man found in America was
   a) A victim of early electrical experiments
   b) A scientific hoax
   c) A victim of a volcanic eruption

5  Scientists learned more about heredity by doing breeding
   experiments with
   a) Coffee beans
   b) Kangaroos
   c) Garden peas

6   One microbe causes one disease was proved by a doctor looking at
    a) Sick chickens
    b) Sick cows
    c) Sick children

7   An enormous collection of dinosaur bones was made by
    a) Cope and Marsh
    b) Hertz and Marconi
    c) An ambitious dog

8   X-rays were discovered by
    a) Henri Becquerel
    b) Wilhelm Konrad Röntgen
    c) Guglielmo Marconi

9   Special effects in cinema were the result of
    a) A shaky cameraman
    b) A snarl-up in the film
    c) An unknown ray

10  A coelacanth is
    a) A seal for champagne bottles
    b) An antibiotic
    c) A living fossil

# THE HUNT FOR UNKNOWN ANIMALS

Some scientists are searching African swamps for a possible surviving dinosaur that local people call *molele-mbembe*. Others delve into Loch Ness in search of living plesiosaurs (the Loch Ness monster?). And others continue to look for a real animal that might have fed legends about ape-like creatures known as the yeti – the abominable snowman from Tibet – and the Bigfoot in Canada. One day, who knows?

## A MIRACLE MOULD

On a September morning in 1928, some young scientists in a hospital laboratory in London, bent over their work, were interrupted by a fellow scientist who often wandered in to see how things were going. This time he was holding a small flat dish (the kind used for growing microbes) with an air of carrying something more than usually interesting. They all had a look, but didn't really concentrate ...

It was only fourteen years later that they understood it was their first sight of a miracle mould that would change the face of medicine for all time. The scientist with the 'interesting' dish, Alexander Fleming, had seen something that they hadn't.

He had been sifting through old dishes with microbes growing on a kind of jelly on them. He was preparing to clean them, chatting all the while with an assistant, Pryce. The two of them had been growing common and very dangerous microbes called *staphylococci*, taken from boils, abscesses, nose and throat and skin infections, leaving them at room temperature to see how they changed, if they grew weaker or stronger. Fleming aimed to find a way to kill harmful microbes.

He inspected the dishes and piled most of them into disinfectant for cleaning. He picked one from the top of the pile, not yet covered by disinfectant. Then he paused, murmured, 'That's funny,' and passed it to Pryce. Pryce saw the usual smooth, domelike colonies of golden-yellow staphylococci covering the dish – *except to one side*. There, near the edge, a patch of fluffy mould was growing, and near to this the colonies of staphylococci were transparent. Quite close to the mould, there were *none at all*.

Something had killed vicious staphylococci! Something *seeping from the mould* had poisoned them. That 'something' was penicillin.

As little as 50 years ago millions of children died every year from throat, stomach, brain and bone infections. Hospitals overflowed with people suffering from deadly infections by microbes. Even just a mouth ulcer or a cut on your knee could kill you. Doctors knew how to kill germs outside the body, but these methods always destroyed the tissues of the body as well. Once an infection penetrated inside, all doctors could do was cut out the infected part and hope the infection wouldn't spread.

This doesn't happen any more because we have antibiotics. Penicillin was the first antibiotic – the first substance that could kill microbes inside the body without harming the body itself. It would be ten years before Fleming's *penicillium* mould was transformed into penicillin medicine by a team of scientists in Oxford led by Howard Florey and Ernst Chain. And that was a long story of trial and error in a makeshift factory.

But without Fleming's alert mind to spot the stray mould that landed, quite by chance, one ordinary September day ...

# DRIFTING CONTINENTS?

Jump, Kevin Jump!

AFRICA

The bones of a tusked reptile that lived some 220 million years ago were found in Antarctica in 1969. The fossil wasn't, in itself, so unusual: Edwin Colbert had already found examples of it, a *Lystrosaurus*, a distant ancestor of the hippopotamus. What was extraordinary was that he'd found those examples in Africa – in the Great Karoo desert at the southern tip of Africa – and in central India: that is, he'd found the fossil on *several different continents*. It confirmed an idea that scientists had had for some time: the separate continents we have now were once a *single landmass*.

In the late nineteenth century an Austrian scientist, Eduard Suess, noticed startling similarities in the rocks, minerals and soils of central India, Madagascar and southern Africa. He concluded that those three separate landmasses must once have been part of the same single landmass, a supercontinent. He named it Gondwanaland, after the Gonds, an ancient kingdom from central India. Many years later, a scientist named Alfred Wegener developed the idea of 'continental drift' – that the world's continents were formed when the single continent broke up, and over millions of years the fragments drifted apart.

Scientists were very doubtful about these ideas at first. But the evidence piled up. They began to form a picture of gigantic, movable continental plates that over a very long time created the shape of land and ocean as it is now on Earth. South America, Australia and Antarctica were also once part of Gondwanaland. Colbert's discovery of *Lystrosaurus* fossils in Africa, India and Antarctica was the perfect final proof. If you look at the outline of all of the continents, they still fit roughly into one another, like a loose jigsaw puzzle.

# LUCY — SHORT, STRONG, AND OVER THREE MILLION YEARS OLD

It was a bleached wasteland of rock, gravel and sand. The two men had been looking for fossils for hours, and the temperature was rising close to 40 °C, beyond endurance. So far their haul was a few teeth of a prehistoric horse and an antelope, part of a pig skull and part of a monkey jaw. Now they'd had enough, and they turned for their Land Rover and the drive back to camp, cutting back through a sandy gully. It had been looked at thoroughly before by other members of their fossil-hunting team, but one of the men, Donald Johanson, though hot, dusty and tired now, was feeling lucky, had a hunch, and wanted one last look.

Disappointingly, there still seemed to be nothing there. They turned to go. That was when Johanson spotted a bit of armbone lying on a slope. Then something else – the back of a small skull. A few feet away, part of a thigh-bone. All around – scattered parts of a skeleton.

A single skeleton? A single individual – in bits? Despite the suffocating heat, Johanson and his companion, Tom Gray, jumped up and down howling with delight, until they realised they might step on something in their excitement, and stopped.

The two men were part of a French-American expedition to the Afar desert in Ethiopia. They hoped to find new fossils to add to the developing record of our past journey on the evolutionary path from ape to human (*see* **The Beagle and the finches** *page 59*). The area is rich in fossils because it is an ancient lake bed, now dry and filled with sediments that show the history of the area in layer on layer: a volcano once erupted, leaving volcanic ash in one layer; mud and silt from distant mountains tells there were rivers here once. All this is revealed up the sides of gullies made when new rivers slice through the lake bed and expose the layers. Occasional rain buckets down, and with no vegetation to bind it, the soil gets washed away, leaving fossils trapped in the ancient layers of rock just sticking out of the side of the gullies, or lying, as this skeleton was, on the surface. You can date the fossils by the layer you find them in.

That night in 1974, back at camp, no one went to bed. All through the night they talked about the find. A single individual, 3.5 million years old? They played the tape-recorder, sending the Beatles tune *Lucy in the Sky with Diamonds* echoing across the desert darkness. The name

Lucy stuck. Her scientific name is *Australopithecus afarensis,* which means Southern Ape from Afar, but she is always known as Lucy.

She is the most complete *Australopithecus* skeleton ever found: the shape of the pelvis showed she was female; the shape of the leg bones, hip and knee joints showed she walked upright on two legs. Her teeth showed that she was about twenty years old when she died. She stands barely a metre tall, and was very ape-like, with long arms, short legs and a small brain. This is important, because it showed that there were prehistoric creatures walking tall before they had enlarged brains. That is, they were erect *before* they had developed an advanced intelligence.

# FOOTPRINTS OF THE PAST

Thousands of miles to the south, two adults and a child walked northwards across an African landscape 3.75 million years ago, leaving their tracks in soft volcanic ash. The volcano Sadiman had belched out clouds of hot grey ash over the

countryside; it had cooled, then was moistened by a light rainshower (we know because the raindrops made tiny indents in the ash).

The damp ash took their footprints perfectly. The sun came out and hardened it, so that the ash set hard as cement. Then Sadiman spewed out more ash, covering the tracks. They lay below the ash, perfect in shape, unseen and undisturbed – for nearly four million years.

It is an extraordinary record, uncovered in 1976 by Mary Leakey and her team of fossil hunters at Laetoli in Tanzania. If the light rain hadn't fallen, the ash and the footprints would have blown away. If the rain had been heavier, it would have washed them away. But a perfect combination of events instead left them for her to find. And what they show is that very ancient human-like creatures walked exactly as we do, with a free-striding movement, millions of years ago. They are the earliest prints of *hominids* (*see page 115*): a large individual in front, a smaller one following behind, for some reason walking in the tracks of the larger one, and a youngster. Was it a family group: male, female, child? The young one seems to have skipped beside them, at one point turning to look round. All around

them are tracks of migrating animals – spring hares, guinea fowl, elephants, pigs, rhinos, buffaloes, hyenas, antelopes, baboons and a sabre-toothed tiger.

you've got to make your mark in life

After Mary Leakey's team found the tracks, studied them in detail and made plaster casts of them, they then covered them again to protect them from wind, sun and rain blowing or washing them away.

# HOMINIDS

Question: what is a hominid? Answer: the name scientists have given to an upright-walking, two-legged creature of the family of human-like creatures which includes the earliest forms. It

can be either an extinct ancestor to humans or a relative of humans developing on a separate branch, or a true human, becoming a modern human – the only hominid living on Earth now. All humans are hominids: but not all hominids are humans.

Human evolution started with an ape. Gradually, over a millions of years, some evolved that were less ape-like and more human-like. Scientists haven't yet found enough fossils to tell us what went on during the in-between time, how each type evolved as millions of years went by. But they do know that at some time some stood up on their hind legs, and all of these humans and near humans have been labelled *hominid*.

## THE HOMINID GANG

This is the nickname given to the most skilled team of fossil hunters in the world. They are a team built in Kenya by Mary and Louis Leakey (*see page 114*) and their son, Richard (*page 118*) – about twelve people who for fifteen years (the leader Kamoya Kimeu for over 25 years) have searched vast expanses of East African terrain for bone and stone treasures from the world's prehistoric past. They have found 200 hominid

fossils, including many skulls, and over 14,000 fossils of other kinds. One of their greatest finds was the *Homo erectus* skeleton, Turkana Boy (*see below*).

## ON TWO LEGS AND LESS APE-LIKE

Scientists now think that the first human species evolved about seven million years ago. But they still don't know how many human species lived and died before one called *Homo erectus* appeared: at least six have been discovered, but perhaps there were twice as many. They do know that all human species before *Homo erectus* walked on two legs but were very ape-like, with small brains.

*Homo erectus* roamed Africa, Europe, China and Malaysia up until about 400,000 years ago, when it disappeared. We know about it mainly from fossil skulls that have been found, and the Turkana Boy skeleton.

## TURKANA BOY

How and why he came to die will probably always remain a mystery. He was barely nine years old when, 1.6 million years ago, his life

ended by the edge of a lake. In the late summer of 1984, Richard Leakey and the Hominid Gang (*see page 116*) were exploring the western shore of Lake Turkana in Kenya. Kamoya Kimeu's sharp, experienced eyes spotted a tiny fragment of an ancient skull lying among pebbles on a slope near a narrow gully recently cut by a new stream. The search lasted over seven months; 1500 tonnes of sediment were moved, sifted and searched. By the time it was over, they had uncovered the most complete skeleton of *Homo erectus* ever found – all in fragments, but enough to reconstruct the whole. Nothing as complete as this has ever been found – other fairly complete skeletons date from a mere 100,000 years ago.

Most experts believe *Homo erectus* originated in East Africa, and then dispersed northwards, throughout Europe and Asia, during the next million years. Their fossils tell us that the adults were thick-boned, massive-jawed, with heavy eyebrow ridges. They had smaller brains than ours but, compared with earlier species we know about, their brains were bigger, faces flatter and bodies more athletic. *Homo erectus* was the first to use fire, the first that could run as modern humans do. But scientists still don't

generally agree on whether *Homo erectus* was our direct ancestor, a side-branch or rival that died out, or none of these. Despite all the finds, it'll take many more relics of human prehistory before scientists can claim they really know the details of the path we took from an ape-like creature to what we are now. It's a field for many more exciting discoveries by fossil hunters the world over ...

# HIDDEN WORLD

Pale crabs, clams, giant white tube worms and sea spiders inhabit a hidden world near cracks in the sea bed that give off volcanic heat from inside the Earth. When they were discovered in the 1980s on the floor of the Pacific Ocean, these animals exploded some important ideas: scientists had believed that living creatures could not survive in pitch darkness more than 2500 metres down – far removed from the energy given by the Sun. But these creatures depend only on volcanic heat and minerals in the water. So these hidden colonies of animals are making scientists rethink some of their ideas about the necessary conditions for life ... and possible ideas about how life began on Earth.

# Teamwork

Many discoveries have emerged from teams of people who come together to pool their knowledge and skills. Many other discoveries — particularly in the past — were made by people working alone.

But even those who worked alone are really part of a team: every scientist builds on the work of all who have gone before. Our knowledge of the world and the forces in it has been gathered over thousands of years, pieced together by different people, working in different ways, at different times — and for different reasons. As scientists tell one another about their work, each can add something to the growing body of knowledge, each can make an important contribution to the whole.

And so science advances — a jigsaw puzzle built piece by piece, the picture becoming clearer and clearer as each new discovery is put in place. This book is full of stories about people who have taken another's discovery and with curiosity explored onwards, opening unexpected doors to their own discovery. There is always someone, somewhere, some time, who will add a tiny — or a large — piece to the jigsaw and take the world forward to new understanding. It is probably happening at this very moment.

# SONS OF THE PHARAOH?

They were buried 3200 years ago – but modern DNA testing may tell us just who they are (*see* **But what are they?** *page 73*). Four skeletons were discovered in April 1997 in the Valley of the Kings in Egypt. There, in the desert valley filled with the rock-hewn tombs of ancient Egyptian rulers and officials, in what had been dismissed as an uninteresting hole in the ground, scientists found a tomb dedicated to the sons of the Pharaoh Rameses II. His reign stretched 67 years from 1279 BC to 1212 BC, and he built more monuments than any other pharaoh. He also fathered at least 50 sons, and names about 100 of his children (from different mothers) on tombs and temple walls.

Researchers had to crawl over rubble from flash floods happening over 3000 years – fragments of the past all mixed up in it – to explore the labyrinth of corridors and chambers. Ancient Egyptians believed a tomb was the home of the dead person's spirit throughout eternity, and so they made it comfortable with furnishings, luxuries, everyday items and pet animals.

Pictures on the walls of this tomb show Rameses and many of his children after death, in the afterlife, and in a pit just inside the entrance to the tomb, they found the bones of four young adult males.

Scientists plan to recover some DNA – the chemical that genes are made of – from these bones. Using recently-developed techniques, they will see if there is a genetic link between the four skeletons – a match in their DNA. If there is, they are probably four of Rameses' sons pictured on the walls.

So here is a twentieth-century discovery – DNA and DNA testing – giving us the chance to look afresh at the discoveries of the past.

Discovery never ends. Each new find adds to the discoveries of the past and opens a door to discovery in the future.

That, really, is what this book is all about.

# Quiz

1   Alexander Fleming found the mould *penicillium*
    a) On a dead fish in his laboratory
    b) In his cheese sandwich
    c) While doing the washing up

2   'Lucy' is at least
    a) 3000 years old
    b) 3,500,000 years old
    c) 35,000 years old

3   *Lystrosaurus* is found on several continents because
    a) It's a very good swimmer
    b) It's a result of spontaneous generation
    c) The continents were once joined

4   Among the discoveries of the nineteenth century were
    a) Champagne
    b) Radioactivity
    c) Microbes

5   Radio was invented following research into
    a) X-rays
    b) Sound waves
    c) Electromagnetic waves

Scientists are rethinking their ideas about the necessary conditions
for life as a result of
a) Fruit-fly experiments
b) Footprints found in Africa
c) Creatures that live in the deep ocean

Rameses was
a) A pharaoh
b) A dinosaur
c) A Greek philosopher

Ancient footprints found near a volcano in Africa came from
a) Bigfoot
b) *Lystrosaurus*
c) Hominids

Radium was used for
a) Marconi's radio transmitter
b) Treating cancer
c) Sailors' compasses

DNA is
a) A curse found in an Egyptian tomb
b) An electrical current produced by a battery
c) A chemical found in living things

# Quiz Answers

**PAGE 49**

1 - c,    2 - b,    3 - a,    4 - b,    5 - c,
6 - c,    7 - a,    8 - c,    9 - b,    10 - a

**PAGE 103**

1 - c,    2 - a,    3 - b,    4 - b,    5 - c
6 - b,    7 - a,    8 - b    9 - b,    10 - c

**PAGE 124**

1 - c,    2 - b,    3 - c,    4 - b,    5 - c,
6 - c,    7 - a,    8 - c,    9 - b,    10 - c

# Index